Sarah's Journey

The story of a Hutterite woman

Debbie Stahl & Melissa Wollman

© 2014 Debbie Stahl & Melissa Wollman

Box 40 • MacGregor, MB • R0H 0R0 • Canada
P. 204-272-5132 • F. 204-252-2381

Cover design: Yvonne Parks

ISBN 978-1-927913-20-8

Library and Archives Canada Cataloguing in Publication

Stahl, Debbie, 1968-, author
    Sarah's journey : the story of a Hutterite woman / Debbie Stahl and Melissa Wollman.

Includes bibliographical references and index.
ISBN 978-1-927913-20-8 (pbk.)

    1. Stahl Wollman, Sarah, 1863-1950. 2. Hutterite women--Canada--Biography. I. Wollman, Melissa, 1984-, author II. Title.

BX8129.H8S73 2014   289.7'3   C2014-903097-5

Printed and bound in Canada.

Table of Contents

'Besorge Ankela' 1
On the Steppes of the Ukraine 3
Voyage to North America 7
Settling in the New Land 9
Move to Wolf Creek 15
Sarah's Letter 17
World War I 21
Rosebud, Alberta 23
Sagebrush and Sandhills 25
Journey Completed 27
Bibliography 29
Appendix I: Family Tree 31
Appendix II: Sarah Wollman's Letter 39
Appendix III: Photos 41

Acknowledgements

We would like to thank all who contributed to recording the story of Sarah Stahl Wollman. In particular, we acknowledge our parents and family, for their support and encouragement.

Tony Waldner of Forest River Community in North Dakota, Ian Kleinsasser of Crystal Spring Community in Manitoba, and E. Annie Walter of Prairie Elk Community in Montana are dedicated to preserving Hutterite history. They generously gave their time and expertise; their help was invaluable and greatly appreciated.

J. Barbara Hofer of Hillview in Alberta, J. Rachel Wurz of Arrowood in Alberta, and Jake S. Stahl of Stanfield Community in Oregon are grandchildren and great-grandchildren of Sarah who shared their memories and helped bring this story to life.

We are grateful to Delsie Hofer, Huron, South Dakota, who turned out to be a long-lost relative and graciously shared stories and pictures of our common ancestors.

Norman Hofer of Freeman, South Dakota, provided us with the Prairieleut perspective and a vivid picture of Hutterite life in the Ukraine.

To the Hutterian Brethren Book Centre, MacGregor, Manitoba, we extend many thanks for providing us with the opportunity to share our rich heritage with a wider audience. We appreciate Dora Maendel's numerous suggestions which greatly enhanced *Sarah's Journey*.

Finally, to all, too numerous to name, who expressed interest and encouraged us to write this story. We hope this effort will inspire many more Hutterites to discover for themselves the amazing history of our people and record other stories, of which there are so many, for future generations to enjoy and learn from.

Debbie Stahl, 2013
Deerfield Colony
Lewistown, Montana

Melissa Wollmann, 2013
Lost River Colony
Allan, Saskatchewan

'BESORGE ANKELA'

The children in our family grew up with the story of our great-great grandmother 'Besorge Ankela'. We were told of the mysterious disappearance of her husband, how she was left alone on the South Dakota prairies with three children, and how she later joined the Hutterian community of Wolf Creek, South Dakota; at the invitation of her brother. The story would invariably finish with: "And children, that's why you're in the *Gma* today!"

However, the telling always left us with many questions. As we sought answers, a woman called Sarah emerged from those stories of the past, giving a clearer picture of the woman she was and the times she lived in.

Sarah was a child in a Ukrainian village, a teenage girl crossing the ocean to a new life in America, a hopeful young wife, mother of three, and a single parent, living in a time of great change for her people, the Hutterites.

This is her story.

The S.S. Mosel, shown here in 1877, is the ship that brought Sarah and her family to North America.

On the Steppes of the Ukraine

Sarah Stahl was born on July 19, 1863 in the Ukraine, a country in Eastern Europe, north of the Black Sea. She was the seventh child of Paul and Kathrina Stahl and grew up in a village called Johannesruh, one of five Hutterite villages in the Ukraine.

Johannesruh had been named after Johann Cornies, a Mennonite whom the Russian government had appointed to oversee the Hutterites. Johannesruh, which Cornies designed, was arranged in the orderly fashion of the Mennonite villages there, with sturdy brick houses on either side of a wide main street. A masonry fence enclosed the front yards of the homes, which were beautiful with flower gardens, and with ash and fruit trees. The entrance to each yard was a gate with brick pillars. The doors of the houses opened to the sides, and if the doors in every house on the street stood open, you could see clear through to the end of the village.

Barns, often added onto the houses, and grain storage were in the back farmyard, looking out over the vast Ukrainian plains known as steppes. Rich black topsoil, up to six feet deep, and the temperate climate made this area some of the best farmland in the world. The fertile soil yielded many bushels of wheat to the hardworking villagers.

Each family had its own plot of land, as well as milk cows and other farm animals. They shared some seasonal work such as seeding and harvesting. Every day one person would take all the milk cows to pasture. In the evening the herder would bring them all home again. The cows plodded down the broad street of the village and each cow would turn off at its own yard for the evening milking. It was a great embarrassment if you overslept and didn't have your cow milked and waiting when the herder came through the village at dawn.

On Sundays, Sarah and her family joined the other villagers in the *Lehrstubm* where the minister read the *Leadn* that the Hutterites had brought with them as they fled from country to country in pursuit of religious freedom. Throughout their journeys through many lands, they had always brought along their faith and history. Ukraine was now the place where they listened to the sermons their ancestors had written, sang their traditional church and martyr songs, and sought to live a life pleasing to God—a life worthy of the many sacrifices their ancestors had made in order to be true to the faith.

At this time, most Hutterite families, including Sarah's family, did not practice community of goods. This had been abandoned several times before due to persecution, internal conflict and theological differences. Community of goods in the Ukraine was originally practiced only in Hutterdorf, where both the Dariusleut and Schmiedeleut had their beginnings. Johannesruh was where the Lehrerleut lived. There, after a brief attempt at community of goods in which they had difficulty convincing their women to participate, they peacefully returned to private ownership.

Sarah's father died in 1867, when she was just four years old, leaving behind a widow and six surviving children. A few years later, Kathrina Stahl remarried, to Johannes Wipf, the widower of her sister-in-law Anna. Within a few years, Sarah had two half-siblings, Jacob and Maria.

In 1870, when Sarah was seven, whispers of change filled the peaceful village. The Russian Tsar, Alexander II, decreed that nobody would be exempt from military duty anymore. The Hutterites, as well as the Mennonites, were told they must obey the new law or leave.

"Leave our villages," people asked. "Our farms, houses and yards? Where will we go?"

"America, America," was the answer. "In America we can have freedom."

Within three years of the Tsar's decree, two Hutterites, Prediger Paul Tschetter and his uncle Lorenz Tschetter accompanied a group of Mennonite delegates to investigate the prairie regions of this new land. They returned with a favourable report, and preparations to move began.

In 1874, the first ship bearing the Schmiedeleut and Dariusleut

Hutterites left for America. On board the Hammonia were many of Sarah's friends and relatives, as well as the boy who would become her future husband—Franz Wollman, who was fourteen years old at the time of immigration. Darius Walter, the founder of Wolf Creek Community near Olivet, South Dakota, was also among the passengers. Paul and Zacharias Wollman, ancestors of the Schmiedeleut Wollmans and second cousins of Franz were on board, as well as Daniel Wollman, a cousin of Franz's father and the ancestor of the Ayers/Ponteix branch of the Dariusleut Wollmans. The Hammonia can be said to have brought most of the Hutterite Wollmans into the New World.

Back in the Ukraine, the Hutterite villages were slowly emptying, the families selling their properties and preparing for their great journey over the sea. They resumed the journey their ancestors had begun over three centuries earlier in the mountains of Tyrol, this time to the 'New World', North America. Only a few Hutterite families chose to stay. Of those, some were too poor to pay for the passage, while others had intermarried with Mennonites.

In 1882, the Mosel was sunk when it ran aground near Cornwall, England.

Voyage to North America

In 1879, Sarah's family left Johannesruh as part of the last Hutterite group to leave the Ukraine. They travelled by train to the harbour of Bremen, Germany where they boarded the ship *Mosel*, joining their fellow Hutterites on the exodus to America. On board were many of Sarah's relatives, also from Johannesruh, including her mother's brother, Michael Hofer, known as *Rutschild*. He lived to be 103 years old, and is buried in the cemetery of Hutterthal Mennonite Church near Freeman, South Dakota.

Two days after Sarah's sixteenth birthday, the ship arrived in New York harbour. As the passengers entered the bustling city teeming with immigrants of different creeds and tongues, their new life in the 'melting pot' of America had begun. They surely must have wondered whether they would be able to keep their faith, their culture and their identity in this strange new world.

By train the Hutterites travelled to Yankton, Dakota Territory and from there by oxcart further north to Freeman. Although the main reasons for leaving Russia had been the government's edicts, some Hutterite leaders also felt that the Mennonite influence was too strong. They looked upon this migration as a chance to escape what they felt was a detrimental influence on the Hutterite people. However, on arrival in Dakota Territory, they found they had little choice but to settle in places where Mennonites would be their nearest neighbours.

The majority of Hutterites had lived non-communally in the Ukraine, and about the same percentage did so in America. For those who wished to live communally, three communities were established. *Prediger* Darius Walter and his congregation established at Wolf Creek, Olivet, while Michael Waldner, *Schmied-Michl Vetter*, and his congregation established Bon Homme Community near Tabor. Jacob Wipf founded a third community, Elm Spring near Ethan. These three communities became known as the Dariusleut, the Schmiedeleut and the Lehrerleut, respectively. Two thirds of the Hutterites chose to homestead and live in private ownership. They believed it was possible to practise the Hutterite faith without literal community of goods. They became known as the Prairieleut.

Most of Sarah's immediate family did not choose communal living. Only her brother Johannes eventually joined Wolf Creek Community, adding his two 160-acre parcels of land to the community's. Sarah's mother and step-father took a homestead near the James River, about two miles east of Wolf Creek Community, and two miles west from where Tschetter Community was later established. Sarah's sister Kathrina, who had married Paul C. Gross in the Ukraine, homesteaded three miles north of the Wolf Creek Community.

Settling in the New Land

During the first years, the settlers faced many difficulties. Unlike the well-cultivated Ukrainian soil, the virgin prairie sod of South Dakota had to be ploughed up and developed. Stone picking was a constant chore. The Ukraine had been quite temperate, with mild winters. Dakota winters were harsh, and given to sudden snowstorms. Frightening tornados and fierce lightning and hail storms came with the heat of summer. Grasshoppers damaged the crops and snakes hiding in the long prairie grasses were a threat.

Also, the Hutterites had never lived on individual farms before. In the Ukraine even those who had not lived communally had been part of villages, which consisted of close-knit families. In America, the Hutterites who chose to live in private ownership lived on scattered homesteads where life was often difficult and harsh.

The new immigrants worked long and hard to create homes for themselves and their families in this new land. They built their first houses out of sod on the treeless plains, even as they thought longingly of the brick houses, fruit trees and fertile fields they had abandoned in the Ukraine. The non-communal Hutterites met in each other's homes for worship and had much fellowship with the communal Hutterites since they shared the same unique beliefs, background and sermons. Most had siblings, parents or even children who had chosen to live on either side of the communal/non-communal divide.

Sunday afternoons were for visiting, and the settlers often visited their relatives in the communities on these afternoons, travelling in ox-drawn carts. Like the others, Sarah, had close familial ties to the communities. Darius Walter, the founder of Wolf Creek Community, was her cousin; and her *Vetter*, Benjamin Stahl had five children

Andreas Wallman, heir to the Wallman-Lepp factory and uncle of Frank Wollman, with wife Maria Nicholls. PHOTO COURTESY OF HERMANN WALLMANN.

who joined Wolf Creek. Her step-father had three brothers at Elm Spring Community, including the founder, Jacob Wipf.

On March 21, 1880 Sarah was baptized into the Neu Hutterthaler Church, Bridgewater, South Dakota by Prediger Paul Tschetter, one of the two Hutterite delegates who had travelled to the New World in 1873 to investigate its possibilities as a homeland for their people.

The family of Franz Wollman—whom Sarah would later marry—also homesteaded. Franz was a dashing young man. He loved making his team of horses prance as he drove his buggy down the main street of Freeman, causing the young ladies to look at the handsome driver. One young lady especially caught his eye, Sarah Stahl.

Sarah married Franz in 1882. Over the next few years, they had three children. Kathrina was born in 1883, Jacob in 1884 and Frank in 1886.

When his youngest son was eight months old, Franz made a decision that affected the future of his family forever. Franz had a rich uncle in Russia, Andreas Wallmann, part owner of an implement factory known as Lepp and Wallmann. Andreas' second marriage had been to a Mennonite girl, Kathrina Lepp, and he had chosen to remain in Russia when the Hutterites moved to North America. However, Andreas had helped finance their journey. Now, several years later, he notified his kin in America that he had money that was available to them if they needed it. Franz Wollman decided to make the journey to borrow money. He bade his family good-bye and set off for Russia to his uncle—but he never returned!

From Russia, Franz wrote letters home to his wife, telling of how he longed to come home and be with her

HUTTERITE MENNONITE CENTENNIAL COMMITTEE

and the children again. He especially longed to see *ma klans Franzela*, my little Frankie. Sarah kept these letters for many years afterwards, and a granddaughter who read them remembers them as being "real love letters."

The last known letter was posted from Vienna, Austria, in July 1887, wherein Franz wrote his wife that he was ill. This was the last Sarah ever heard from her husband. Later, a trunk containing a large Russian fur coat and some money was forwarded to Sarah by a hotel in New York, but she received no further news of him.

A ship list indicates that Franz Wollman departed from Bremen, Germany, on the ship *Trave* and arrived in New York on August 19, 1887. Investigations by his uncle Andreas showed that Franz returned to New York with the money and purchased a train ticket to Freeman, but that was as far as he could trace him. Soon the Hutterite communities and the surrounding area swirled with rumours of the young man who had so mysteriously disappeared.

"He must've bragged about the money he had," some said, "And the wrong people heard him."

"Always proud, that one!" others declared. "I knew something like that would happen."

"Maybe it was the gold watch chain he always wore around his neck," some speculated. "Could be he let it hang out and somebody saw it!"

None of the rumours were ever proven to be true. Franz had vanished completely and inexplicably.

Sarah, just 23 years old and left alone with three children, returned to her parents' homestead near the James River where she lived for the next six years. In all this time she never gave up hope that someday her husband would return. A family picture taken at this time shows Sarah with the youngest child in her lap and the other two by her side. She gazes from the photos with an air of quiet resignation and strength.

Franz's siblings and his parents left for Canada two years after their son's disappearance. His brother Joseph settled near Nipawin, Saskatchewan with his wife Susie Janzen and their family.

Sarah stayed with her parents but worried for her children. They were growing and needed schooling, but the local school was too far away for them to attend. She waited to hear news of her husband and wondered what to do next.

Then, one night, Sarah had a dream. She was walking through a dark forest, leading her children by the hand. Darkness was all around her but in the distance she saw a light. Hastening toward it, she found it led her out of the wood to the Wolf Creek Community.

Sarah Stahl Wollman with her three children: Frank, Kathrina, and Jacob.

The next morning she told her mother about the dream and asked her what it could mean. Her mother replied, "Dear daughter, it means the light for you and your children is at Wolf Creek. Go and join them. Your brother has asked you often enough."

Her mind made up, Sarah prepared to moved to the community with her children.

Wolf Creek Community, South Dakota, ca. 1920s.

Move to Wolf Creek

At this time, both the community people and the Prairieleut still referred to themselves and each other as Hutterites. Their ministers exchanged sermons with one another and there was considerable interaction, with some communitarians leaving for the prairie and prairie-folk joining the communities. Therefore, Sarah was not re-baptized when she joined Wolf Creek Community, but was accepted upon her confession of faith and the laying on of hands. Her first baptism by a non-communitarian Hutterite minister was considered valid.

Over time, as the Dariusleut population grew, more communities were established in South Dakota. Besides farming, they ran flour-mills, herded cattle and sheep, and produced flocks of geese and ducks. Trades practiced by Hutterite men included carpentry, broom making, shoemaking, blacksmithing, and bookbinding. From their bountiful gardens the women filled root cellars with potatoes. They dried peas and corn to eat in the winter. Sometimes they shared their garden produce with their Prairieleut relatives.

Sarah liked community life but she often felt lonely and cried when she thought of her missing husband. In her great need, she prayed to God and asked for a sign that she might know if he was alive or dead. That night, she felt a cold hand pressed against her forehead and took it as a sign that he was dead.

Over the years, Sarah received marriage proposals but the elders told her: "No, you cannot marry because we do not know if your husband is living or not."

Around 1900, Sarah's mother and step-father died within a year of each other and they were buried near their homestead on the banks of the James River. Their son Jacob (nicknamed Knox) Wipf and his family lived in the wooden, two-storey house constructed by his parents. The house had been built into a hillside on the homestead. Like his father before him, Jacob farmed the land.

In 1906, Sarah wrote a letter to Elisabeth Martens in Russia, her husband's *Tante*, who had asked for news of his family. The letter was published in *Die Mennonitische Rundschau*, a Mennonite periodical. She wrote of her decision to join the Hutterian community, where "each Sunday and evening church service could bring me comfort," and where her children could attend school. Almost twenty years had passed since her husband disappeared, yet she still hoped for some news of him. Her deep sadness is apparent in her letter, but she wrote that the dear Saviour helped her carry the burden.

Sarah's Letter[1]

Dear Editor,

Please publish my letter in the columns of the Rundshau.

May the grace of our Lord Jesus Christ be with us, and you all! Dear friends, because you are anxious to hear news of your friends, I am willing to write a reply. In the Rundshau, *I read that you asked my husband's aunt, Elisabeth Martens, about my missing husband, Franz Wollman, and that you have asked whether my children could give any news of their father. My poor children don't even know their father and likewise don't know anything about him. I have three children, one daughter, Katharina and two sons, Jacob and Franz. The daughter knows a little bit about her father as she was four years old at the time, but the sons don't know anything about their father as one was only three years old and the youngest only eight months. It has been with great difficulty that I raised my children amid sorrow and a troubled spirit, but thanks be to God, they are good and obedient. The other women often told me, "You have good children."*

Pentecost is once more at hand and still I know nothing. All my hopes, all my desires and all my efforts have been unsuccessful and it is with a heavy heart that I look towards the future. The awareness of having a husband and not knowing whether he is dead or alive often almost breaks my heart! Now I, Sarah Wollman, deeply grieved wife, will tell you about my husband Franz. Up until this day, I still have found or heard no news or trace of him, where he

---

1 *Mennonitishe Rundshau*, May 23, 1906. Translated by Ian Kleinsasser, Crystal Spring Community, Manitoba.

might be or whether he is alive or dead—which is known only to God. If he had died here, I would know and would have buried him, but now I know nothing and cannot get him out of my mind or thoughts. Some people say he is dead, some say he is alive and could be living somewhere, but if so, he has not let us know. Thus, I won't believe until I see him with my own eyes. Oh, how gladly I would hear some information regarding him! I'm sure everyone can imagine how heartrending it is, but only those it affects, can truly feel it. For many years now I have had a heavy heart and spirit so that if the dear Saviour would not have helped me, I could not have carried through with it. But God is gracious and merciful towards his children who love and trust Him, and helps them to overcome.

Nineteen years and six months have now passed since my Franz left for Russia and never returned. A number of years ago, his uncle, Andreas Wollman, informed me that Franz made it to New York where he purchased a ticket for Freeman, but he never left. So possibly he stayed in the evil city. The proverb speaks well which says: "No thread is woven so fine and there is no secret that will not be revealed" but with regard to this sad story, so far nothing has come to light. Please, if anyone knows anything about him, could you tell me or let me know!

Your brother Jacob [Knels] along with his three children, is in the community. Two of his sons are married and the youngest one is still single. Both he and his wife [Sarah Gross] already look old. This spring, they, as well as sixteen other families, moved a 100 miles away to Beadle County where they established a new community, [Huron Community] Your mother [Susanna Wollman, sister to Frank Wollman, SR] and your sisters Susanna and Katharina are no longer alive. Your brother Abraham lives a long way from us, namely, in Manitoba, Canada. The Dariusleut have also established a community in South Dakota next to the Wolf Creek. My Uncle Darius [founder of the Dariusleut] is no longer alive either. In July it will be three years since he passed away. His wife, Onge, [Anna] is still living. His parents passed away 16 years ago. His brother Jacob Walter also passed away quite suddenly two years ago of a stroke, but his wife is still alive. I too am living in community with my children, namely with the Dariusleut. I have now lived 14 years in the community. In material things, my life is good. We have enough of everything. Only the one thing is missing and this is that I do not know the whereabouts of my husband. When my husband left for Russia I was 23 years old and as of the 19th of July, I will be 43 years old. With God's help, I have until now lived my young life alone and in loneliness. The first six years I lived with my parents on the farm. My children were growing up and needed to be schooled but the school was far away. So, after earnest deliberation, I moved to the community with my children where each vesper and Sunday church service could bring me comfort. My children attended school and were quick to learn. Four years and six months ago my daughter married a certain Jacob Wurz. She has three children: one son and two daughters. Last January, my Jacob was married to my Uncle Jacob Walter's daughter, Elizabeth. My youngest son is still single. He is 20 years old.

Dear Aunt [Elizabeth], I recently read in the Rundshau about Moses Stahl. The dear uncle is no longer alive. He passed away quite a while ago. He was my father's brother, namely Paul Stahl. My dear father passed away a long time ago. He passed away while yet in Russia. At the time, I was only a child of five years. My dear mother then married her brother-in-law, Johann Wipf. They both passed away five years ago. They died only a year apart. David Waldner is still alive, but his wife has already passed away. He is presently living in Manitoba, Canada with his youngest son. He only had two sons. Johann Wurz is also still alive and has been married twice. He is also living in a brotherhood community [Old Elm] and lives only 15 miles from us. His children, from his marriage to your sister, are all married except for his youngest daughter.

I close my humble letter and greet you all, dear aunt as well as your husband and children.

I remain your nephew's deeply grieved wife,

Sarah Wollman

WORLD WAR I

The onset of the First World War in 1914 brought many problems for the Hutterites. Their English-speaking neighbours looked suspiciously on these German-speaking settlers, and were not pleased that they refused to fight or to support the war in any way. Some residents of the Yankton area stole one hundred cattle and a thousand sheep from the Jamesville Community where Sarah was now living and sold them in order to donate the proceeds to the war effort.

The United States Government did not grant the communal Hutterites or the Prairieleut conscientious objector status, and in 1917 some of their young men were drafted. In addition to scores of Hutterite men kept at Fort Riley, Kansas; four Lehrerleut Hutterite men from Rockport Community at Alexandria, SD, were court-martialed at Fort Lewis, in Washington State, and sentenced to thirty-seven years imprisonment. Their hands and feet chained together, they were transferred by rail to Alcatraz Prison in California. Here they suffered several months of harsh treatment including inhumane beatings and were eventually transferred to Fort Leavenworth, Kansas, where they arrived exhausted and demoralized. Two of the young men, Joseph and Michael Hofer, died as a result of the brutal treatment they received.

Once again, the Hutterites faced the question: Should they leave their homes and farms behind in order to be able to do what they believed was right? The answer was the same as before: Yes.

As a result, Dariusleut leaders went to search for suitable farmland in Canada. The Canadian government had promised them exemption from military service and the right to hold their land in common, as well as other privileges.

By this time, Sarah's children were grown and married. Her son-in-law Jacob Wurz, who was the Prediger at Jamesville Community, went looking for land in Alberta along with other Hutterite leaders. They purchased land near Rockyford, northeast of Calgary. In the fall of 1918, the Jamesville Community sold its land in South Dakota and moved to new land in Canada. The financial cost of this move was formidable, because the Hutterites had to sell their land for much less than it was worth.

Sarah, along with her children Kathrina and Frank, as well as their families, were among the Hutterites who made the long train ride to their new home. From South Dakota they travelled to Minneapolis, Minnesota; and from there up to Winnipeg, Manitoba. Leaving Winnipeg, they crossed the prairie provinces, Manitoba and Saskatchewan, and arrived in Calgary, Alberta. What must Sarah have felt as she left behind yet another home to travel to a new country?

Rosebud, Alberta

Their new home in Alberta, Springvale Community, had wide open fields of cropland with rich soil, well suited for farming. The Rosebud Creek ran past the community, alongside of which grew clusters of wild poplar, willow, saskatoon berry and chokecherry trees. The women and girls picked the fruit and used it to make wine. Chokecherries were also dried and then boiled with leftover *Samstig Tee* for a special treat on Saturday evenings in winter. Sarah lived with her daughter Kathrina and her family. She faithfully performed her community duties and helped out wherever she could.

Meanwhile, back in the Ukraine, the Russian Revolution of 1917 was taking a terrible toll on the Mennonites and the few Hutterites who had remained behind. The communities of Johannesruh and Hutterthal were attacked, and many people lost their lives. Others lost all of their property, and were homeless and hungry. Andreas Wallman, the millionaire heir to the Lepp and Wallman factory, lost the family fortune and factory to the Revolutionists. His family faced terrible persecution because of its wealth. His son, Paul Wallmann, immigrated to Canada and settled in St. Catharines, Ontario. (Through Andreas' descendants, the Wollman (or Wallmann) name was brought among the Mennonites, a number of whom lived in the St. Catharines area.)

Although some Prairieleut had immigrated to Canada, a large number stayed behind in the Dakotas, including most of Sarah's siblings. As the elders had feared, without the boundary of communal life, the Mennonite influence proved to be too strong for the independent Prairieleut churches. After the death of their *Ältester*, Paul Tschetter, in 1919, they stopped reading the ancestral sermons and dropped the German language. Much of the religious and cultural distinctiveness was lost, and all Prairieleut churches eventually joined Mennonite Conferences, calling themselves 'Hutterite Mennonites.'

On the Alberta prairies, the Hutterites worked hard to establish their new communities. Sarah became known as *'Besorge Ankela'* because of the way she cared for others. Springvale, near Rockyford, which was also known as Jamesville after the old place in South Dakota, was rather poor in the early years. Their nearby brethren at Rosebud had received a better price for their land back in South Dakota, and were much more prosperous. People from Jamesville sometimes made trips to Rosebud for shoes and other materials. The *Kutter* (Rosebud) people teasingly nicknamed the Jamesville people *Bethlehemiter* since they often gave them supplies, but this did not effect their generosity. Some of these trips to *Kutter* were made by *Besorge Ankela*, who would then make sure everybody at Jamesville received a fair share of what she brought back.

Sarah's grandchildren remember her as their refuge. One granddaughter recalls that when she ripped her apron, she asked her kind-hearted *Ankela* to mend it so she wouldn't get into trouble at home. Sarah taught some of her grandchildren and great-grandchildren Russian phrases such as *Dobroy Utro*, Good morning, and *Ya Tebya Luybluy*, I love you. She also taught them how to count to ten in Russian: *odin, dva, tre, choture*...patiently repeating until they got it right. The Hutterites of Sarah's generation still spoke very little English, mostly German and Russian.

When the mothers at Springvale left for their home communities to visit their parents, Sarah would help out in their homes while they were gone. She would take arm-loads of mending and do it, and also give a hand with the laundry. Sometimes she travelled to other communities such as Pincher Creek and Stahlville to help her granddaughters with their growing families.

SAGEBRUSH AND SANDHILLS

In 1936, it was time for Sarah to move again. The Springvale Community branched out and established Sandhills Community, fifteen miles west along Rosebud Creek, near the town of Beiseker. Trees and clumps of sagebrush dotted the sand hills after which the community was named, but the farmland was fertile and level. Wild strawberries grew in a sandy pasture south-west of the community, along with crocuses and tiger lilies. The women planted hollyhocks, poppies and bachelor's button in the front yards of the homes, saving the seeds to sow the following year.

Coal-burning stoves warmed the houses. Coal was brought from the mines at Drumheller, and each family had a shack in front of its house to store it. A Booker coal stove with a hot plate stood in the living room. On top of this there was always a kettle of hot water and sometimes a pot of coffee. Much of the water used in the homes was either rainwater or melted snow, depending on the season. Water could also be carried home from the communal kitchen. Smaller stoves which required only a bit of coal stood in the bedrooms. During the day, the front room of their house was often filled with children in their *Wagele*. Sarah and her daughter Kathrina would baby-sit when the mothers had work to do.

When Sarah's granddaughter, Rebecca Wurz married Chris Gross in August 1942, Sarah went to live with another granddaughter, Maria, to make room for the married couple. Finally, she moved in with her son Frank and his family, and here she spent her last years. She received loving care and never had to be alone. A grandson's wife braided her hair on Saturdays, and her great-grandsons refilled the coal bucket for her stove. In the evenings she would sometimes visit her grandchildren and their families, and her great-granddaughters would carefully walk her home again at night.

Journey Completed

In the winter of 1950, Sarah was 86 years old. She had lived to see all of her siblings except Johannes, and many of her relatives, friends and neighbours from the Hutterite villages of the Ukraine move far away from their roots. She had been left alone with three children at the age of 23 and had lived widowed, yet not widowed for 63 years. She had lived to see her children's children, yes, even to the third generation.

One day that winter, her family sensed the end was near, so they sat by Sarah's bedside—her daughter, sons, grandchildren, even a great-granddaughter. They watched as Sarah folded and lifted her hands, as if in prayer.

"She wants us to pray," someone whispered. They all knelt on the floor in prayer. When they arose, they saw that Sarah had died. Her earthly pilgrimage had ended. A life of devotion and love, of partings and sorrow was over. The girl from Johannesruh in the Ukraine died at the age of 86, surrounded by her family. God had not forsaken the forsaken.

Many relatives and friends from various communities came to the funeral, but no Prairieleut. Most of Sarah's siblings had already died, and the rift between communal Hutterites and their relatives who had chosen to live non-communally was almost complete. Despite their shared ancestry and history, the Hutterites from the Ukraine had separated upon settling in America and the two paths had led in opposite directions.

Sarah's burial took place on a bitterly cold winter's day; the women hung the backs of the vehicles with bed sheets in an attempt to keep warm on the way to the *Friedhof*. The journey begun half a world away and many years before in the village of Johannesruh now came to an end as Sarah was laid to rest in the frozen Alberta earth. The crowd gathered and watched as the coffin was lowered, and the minister gave a brief benediction.

Sarah Wollman left many descendants. Today, most of these live in Hutterite communities in Canada and the United States. Kathrina, her daughter, married Jacob Wurz, who later became Prediger. They had fourteen children, eleven of whom survived. Their descendants can be found in many communities, including Birch Meadows, Alberta; Craigmyle, Alberta; Codesa, Alberta; Eagle Creek, Saskatchewan; Huxley, Alberta; Morinville, Alberta; Mountain View, Alberta; Riverbend, Saskatchewan; Sandhills, Alberta; Stahls, Washington State; Stanfield, Oregon; Viking, Alberta; and Warburg, Alberta.

Sarah's elder son, Jacob, married Elizabeth Walter, daughter of Jacob Walter and his third wife, Maria Kleinsasser Wurz. They had nine children together. He moved along with his wife's family, eventually ending up at Pincher Creek Community in Alberta. Many of his descendants now live in Washington communities. After the death of Jacob's wife in 1941, he married Maria Walter, daughter of Ältester Elias Walter at Standoff. They had one son.

Sarah's younger son, Frank, married Sarah Walter. She died in the Spanish influenza of 1918, leaving five children. Frank then married 22 year old Sarah Tschetter from Standoff, and they had nine more children. Frank's descendants now live at Blue Sky, Alberta; Cluny, Alberta; Hairy Hill, Alberta; Hillcrest, Saskatchewan; Hillview, Alberta; Leask, Saskatchewan; and Lost River, Saskatchewan; among other communities. With inter-marriage and community branch-offs, Franz and Sarah Wollman have descendants in over half of the Dariusleut Hutterite communities.

The legacy Sarah Wollman leaves for her many descendants includes *Gelassenheit*, courage and endurance in the face of hardships, a heart that gave unselfishly to serve others, and unwavering faith and trust in the Lord.

Bibliography

_____. *Dariusleut Hutterite Colony Family Lists 2012*. Revised edition. Compiled by George K. Tschetter. Birch Hills Book Bindery: Birch Hills, 2012.

_____. *Lehrerleut Hutterian Brethren Church Family Records*. Millennium Edition. Compiled By Rev. Joseph J. Hofer, Rimrock Colony: Sunburst, 2002.

_____. *Schmiedeleut Family Record*. Fifth Edition. Compiled by David Gross, Sommerfeld Hutterite Colony: High Bluff, 2009.

Janzen, Rod and Stanton, Max. *The Hutterites in North America*. Baltimore: John Hopkins University Press, 2010.

Janzen, Rod. *The Prairie People*. University Press of New England: Hanover, 1999.

Hiebert, Jerald. *The Hutterite Story of a Pure Church: A Study of Dariusleut Alberta Hutterites 1918-2000*, 3rd edition. Masters disertation, Regent College, 2001.

Hofer, Arnold and Hofer, Norman. *Hutterite Roots*. Eugene: Wipf and Stock Publishers, 2012.

Hofer, Samuel. *Hutterites: Lives and Images of a Communal People*. Hofer Publishers: Saskatoon, 1998.

Hutterite Mennonite Steering Committee, The. *History of the Hutterite Mennonites*. Wipf and Stock Publishers: Eugene, 1975.

Waldner, Johannes. *The Chronicle of the Hutterian Brethren*, Volume Two. Translated by the Hutterian Brethren. Ste. Agathe: Crystal Spring Colony, 1996.

Wurtz, Edna and Masuk, Kathy. *Rooted and Grounded in Love: The History and Family Records of the Langham Prairie People*. Saskatoon, 2000.

APPENDIX I: FAMILY TREE[2]

Ancestry of Frank Wollman

Andreas Wollman (November 20, 1787 - December 13, 1845) [34]

Kathrina Pullman (April 15, 1791) [36]

   Married: November 14, 1807

Susanna (June 22, 1814 - January 1, 1894)
Married to Jacob Knels mentioned in Sarah's letter. Has descendants among Schmiedeleut and Lehreleut.

Franz (November 25, 1815 - August 16, 1822)

Ester (September 12, 1821 - ?)

Franz (July 18, 1824 - 1900) HILLCREST

Jacob (March 22, 1827 - December 20, 1866)
Married: Susanna Wurz [111].

Paul (October 15, 1831)

Andreas (June 12, 1835 - November 10, 1900) [215]
The wealthy uncle from whom Frank borrowed money.

Joseph Miller (September 28, 1793 - August 4, 1859) [45]

Christina Wollman (July 27, 1784 - October 31, 1863) [34]

   Married: January 19, 1815

---

2 Numbers in square brackets refer to the *Russia Records* (Tony Waldner, Forest River Bookbindery. Fordville, 2008.); place names refer to the *Dariusleut Family Records*.

Joseph (May 30, 1820 - April 9, 1823)
Stundel (August 6, 1822); [161]
Kathrina (1824 - July 28); [165]
Sarah or Susanna (November 5, 1826 - October 20, 1918); HILLCREST
Joseph (September 4, 1828 - September 28, 1828)
Anna (September 29, 1829 - September 8, 1831)
Isaak (April 8, 1833 - May 22, 1833)
Jacob (April 8, 1833 - October 20, 1833)
Andreas (October 17, 1834) [212]

Hillcrest:
Frank Wollman (July 18, 1824 - ?) [96]
Sarah Miller (November 5, 1826 - October 20, 1918) [107]
Andreas (January 1, 1851 - ?)
Kathrina (January 1, 1852 - ?)
Joseph (November 29, 1853 - August 8, 1935)
Married Susie Jantzen.
Frank (February 4, 1860 - disappeared in 1886)
Paul (January 1, 1865 - ?)

Ancestry of Sarah Stahl

Johann Stahl (November 1, 1789 - April 8, 1866) [40]
Ester Kleinsasser (March 31, 1793 - ?) [41]
   Married: January 2, 1810
Mose (January 25, 1811 - December 10, 1898) [178]
Benjamin (March 14, 1812 - ?) [148]
Friedrich (June 11, 1815 - January 20, 1816)
Kathrina (January 20, 1817 - August 30, 1891) [141]
Mother of Darius Walter, the first Dariusleut Ältester.
Johann (September 13, 1822) [194]
Paul (June 10 1832 - February 13, 1867) DOWNIE LAKE

Joseph (June 10, 1834 - February 28, 1836)
Anna (December 2, 1836 - ?)
First wife of Johannes Wipf [128].
Joseph (April 1, 1839 - October 6, 1839)
Ester (February 3, 1825 - March 27, 1892) [181-B & 209]

Joshua Hofer (November 10, 1806 - January 24, 1876) [64]
Anna Pullman (May 26, 1808 - ?) [51]
    Married: November 7, 1826
Kathrina (August 6, 1827 -) DOWNIE LAKE
Michael (August 4, 1829 - October 25, 1932)
Prairieleut, known as 'Rutschild'.
Elizabeth (October 4, 1931 - ?)
Justina (August 10, 1834 - ?) [205]
Joshua (January 28, 1837 - ?) RIVERSIDE
David (May 6, 1839 - ?)
Jacob (November 7, 1841 - ?)
Mathias (November 7, 1841 - ?)
Joseph (January 1, 1844 - ?)
Andreas (January 1, 1849 - ?)
Rebecca (March 23, 1851 - ?)
Anna (August 28, 1846 - ?)

Paul Stahl (June 10, 1832 - February 13, 1867) [86]
Kathrina Hofer (August 6, 1827 - ?) [126]
    Married: December 16, 1851
Johannes (September 5, 1852 - October 20, 1852)
Kathrina (January 2, 1854 - January 14, 1947)
Married Paul Gross [156] on October 22, 1872.
Anna (April 15, 1855 - September 18, 1856)
Anna (January 25, 1857 - 1882)
Married Jacob Hofer on October 27, 1874.

Paul (January 13, 1859 - June 23, 1903)
Married Anna Kleinsasser.

Johannes (May 17, 1861 - March 29, 1942) DOWNIE LAKE
Brother who asked Sarah to join him at Wolf Creek, SD.

Sarah (July 19, 1863 - January 22, 1950)

Joshua (September 17, 1865)
Married Barbara Tschetter.

2nd marriage to:

Johannes Wipf (February 4, 1835 - ?) [128]
Widower, his first wife was Anna Stahl [86].

Married: November 2, 1867

Jacob (November 20, 1868 - June 21, 1940)
Married Susanna Glanzer.

Maria (August 1, 1871 - December 23, 1932)
Married Joseph Knells.

Descendants of Frank Wollman and Sarah Stahl

Hillcrest:

Frank Wollman (February 4, 1860 - disappeared 1886) HILLCREST

Sarah Stahl (July 19, 1863 - January 22, 1950) DOWNEY LAKE

Married: May 3, 1882

Kathrina (February 25, 1883 - June 27, 1950) SPRINGVALE

Jacob (June 19, 1884 - August 21, 1963) WARDEN

Frank (February 20, 1886 - May 10, 1966) HILLCREST

Springvale:

Pr. Jacob Wurz (August 7, 1882 - April 26, 1952) SPRINGVALE

Kathrina Wollman (February 25, 1883 - June 27, 1950) HILLCREST

Married: December 1, 1901

Kathrina (November 7, 1902 - May 14, 1984) CRAIGMYLE
Jacob (May 12, 1904 - July 9, 1981) MORINVILLE
Sarah (December 6, 1905 - May 10, 1995) HUXLEY
Johannes (April 16, 1907 - January 17, 1981) BIRCH MEADOWS
Rachel (October 27, 1908 - November 8, 1918)
Susanna (July 17, 1910 - April 19, 1992) WARBURG
Andreas (June 21, 1912 - January 21, 1980) EAGLE CREEK
Maria (August 9, 1914 - May 14, 1996) VIKING
Joseph (July 13, 1916 - April 4, 1989) EAGLE CREEK
Elizabeth (January 30, 1918 - March 7, 1991) MOUNTAIN VIEW
Paul (February 5, 1920 - September 10, 1986) SANDHILLS
Rebecca (June 1, 1921 - November 29, 2003) RIVERBEND
Rachel (April 20, 1924 - April 23, 1924)
Rachel (May 30, 1926 - September 1, 1926)

Warden:
   Jacob Wollman (June 19, 1884 - August 21, 1963) HILLCREST
   Elizabeth Walter (October 20, 1883 - June 12, 1941) STANDOFF
      Married: January 2, 1906
   Paul (January 20, 1907 - January 4, 1925)
   Elias (September 25, 1908 - December 10, 1997) WARDEN
   Maria (November 4, 1910 - April 13, 1981) RED WILLOW
   Sarah (May 9, 1913 - April 1, 1967) ESPANOLA
   Elizabeth (December 17, 1915 - December 29, 1999) ESPANOLA
   Rebecca (December 16, 1917 - October 27, 1918)
   Rebecca (June 26, 1919 -) MARLIN
   Rachel (October 9, 1921 - November 6, 1992) BELLE PLAIN
   Anna (November 15, 1925 - January 16, 2001) SCHOONOVER

2nd Marriage to:
Maria Walter June 6, 1907 - December 10, 1995) STANDOFF
    Married: November 9, 1941
    Joseph (May 18, 1946 -)

Hillcrest:
Frank Wollman (February 20, 1886 - May 10, 1966) HILLCREST
Sarah Walter (August 5, 1885 - October 29, 1918) WEST BENCH
    Married: unknown
    Frank (June 24, 1908 - May 24, 1970) LEASK
    Paul (January 9, 1910 - May 26, 1950) RIVERBEND
    Jacob (April 29, 1912 - November 27, 1986) LEASK
    Joseph (December 2, 1914 - December 8, 1995) HILLCREST
    Maria (January 3, 1917 - March 13, 1917)
    Johannes (May 18, 1918 - August 15, 1921)

2nd Marriage to:
Sarah Tschetter May 23, 1898 - June 16, 1976) MIXBURN
    Married: July 25, 1920
    Michael (July 26, 1921 - November 15, 1974) LOST RIVER
    Barbara (November 2, 1922) HILLVIEW
    Sarah (December 7, 1923 - October 5, 2008) CLUNY
    Johannes (October 25, 1925 - November 6, 1990) HILLCREST
    Peter (November 17, 1929 - August 5, 1943)
    Anna (September 27, 1931 - March 23, 2012) BLUE SKY
    Rachel (March 17, 1933 -) HAIRY HILL
    Elias (June 18, 1936 - October 11, 2007)
    Darius (December 28, 1938 - January 4, 1939)

Appendix II: Sarah Stahl's Letter

Letter written by Sarah Stahl, dated May 5, 1906, requesting information about her missing husband and providing her "Tante Elizabeth Martens" with details about her relatives living in Hutterian communities in Canada. Submitted to the Mennonite periodical, *Die Mennonitische Rundschau*.[3] Published here in the original German.

Werter Editor!

Bitte mein Schreiben in die Spalten der "Rundschau" aufzunehmen. Die Gnade unseres Herrn Jesu Christo sei mit uns und Euch allen.

Liebe Freunde! Dieweil Ihr neugierig seid von Eurer Freundschaft zu hören, so bin ich bereit zu antworten. Ich habe in der „Rundschau" gelesen das Du, meines Mannes Tante, Elisabeth Martens, nach meinen verschollenen Mann, Franz Wallmann, fragtest und daß meine Kinder Euch sollen Nachricht geben von ihrem Vater. Meine armen Kinder kennen ja ihren Vater nicht, und wissen nichts von ihm. Ich habe drei Kinder, eine Tochter Katharina und zwei Söhne, Jakob und Franz. Die Tochter weiß ein wenig von ihrem Vater, sie war vier Jahre alt, die Söhne wissen nichts von ihm, einer war drei Jahre alt; der jüngste war acht Monate alt. Ich habe meine Kinder sehr schwer in Traurigkeit mit einem schweren Gemüht auferzogen, aber Gott sei's gedankt, sie waren artig und folgsam. Die Frauen sagten oft zu mir: Du hast gute Kinder.

---

3 *Mennonitishe Rundshau,* May 23, 1906.

Pfingsten ist wieder vor der Tür, und noch immer nichts erfahren—all mein Hoffen, all mein Verlangen, alle meine Bemühungen, waren bis jetzt erfolglos und mit einem schweren Herzen blicke ich in die Zukunft. Das Bewußtsein einen Mann zu haben und nicht zu wissen, ob tot oder lebendig, bricht mir oft beinahe das Herz! Nun will ich tiefbetrübt Frau, Sarah Wollman, Euch von meinem Mann Franz berichten. Ich habe bis auf den heutigen Tag noch keine Spur und keine Nachricht von ihm wo er geblieben ist, ob er noch wo lebt oder ob er tot ist—das ist allein Gott bekannt; wäre er gestorben, so wüßte ich doch, daß ich ihn begraben hätte, aber jetzt weiß ich nichts, kann ihn nicht aus dem Sinn und Gedanken lassen. Manche Leute sagen er sei tot, manche sagen er lebt—er kann sich wo aufhalten, aber er läßt nichts von sich hören. Das glaube ich nicht eher, bis ich ihn mit meinen leiblichen Augen sehen werde, daß er noch lebt. O wie gerne möchte ich schon Auskunft von ihm haben, denn es kann ja ein jeder denken, wie es einem ums Herz ist, aber es fühlts nur der, den es betrifft. Ich habe ein schweres Herz und Gemüht schon so viele Jahre, wenn's mir der liebe Heiland nicht täte tragen helfen, so könnte ich es nicht durchmachen, aber Er ist ja gnädig und barmherzig gegen seine Kinder, die ihn lieben und ihm vertrauen, denen hilft er ja überwinden.

Es ist jetzt 19 Jahre und 6 Monat[e] da[ß] mein Franz nach Rußland gereist und nicht mehr zurückgekommen ist. Sein Onkel, der Andreas Wallmann hat mir vor vielen Jahren Nachricht gegeben, daß mein Franz ist nach New York gekommen und von dort ein Ticket genommen, um nach Freeman zu fahren, aber abgefahren wäre er nicht. So muß er wahrscheinlich in der bösen Stadt geblieben sein. Das Sprichwort sagt wohl: Es ist kein Faden so fein gesponnen und ist nichts Heimliches, das nicht offenbar wird, aber von der traurigen Geschichte ist bis jetzt noch nichts ans Licht gekommen! Bitte wenn jemand etwas von ihm weiß, der möchte es mir berichten und zu wissen tun.

Dein Bruder Jakob, [Tante Elizabeth], ist mit seinen drei Kindern in der Brüdergemeinde, zwei Söhne hat er verheiratet und der jüngste ist noch ledig, er und seine Frau sehen schon alt aus, sie sind dieses Frühjahr 100 Meilen weitergezogen, sowie auch 16 andere Familien und haben eine Gemeinde angelegt in Beadel County. Deine Mutter und Schwester Susanna und Katharina, sind nicht mehr am Leben. Dein Bruder Abraham ist weit ab von uns, nämlich in Manitoba, Canada mit seinen Kindern und die Dariusleute sind auch in einer Brüdergemeinde in Süddakota an der Wolfskrick [sic]. Mein Darius Vetter ist nicht mehr am Leben; bis im Juli wird es drei Jahre das er tot ist; seine Frau Onge lebt noch. Seine Eltern sind schon 16 Jahre tot. Sein Bruder Jakob Walter ist auch schon zwei Jahre tot, er ist plötzlich gestorben, der Schlag hat ihn gerührt. Seine Frau lebt noch. Ich bin auch in der Gemeinde mit meinen Kindern, nämlich bei den Dariusleute[n]. Ich bin jetzt schon 14 Jahre in der Gemeinde. Im natürlichen Leben geht es mir nichts ab. Wir haben von allem genug, nur das eine fehlt, daß ich nicht weiß[,] wo mein Mann geblieben ist. Als er nach Rußland reiste, war ich 23 Jahre alt und den 19 Juni werde ich 43 Jahre alt. Ich habe also mit Gottes Hilfe mein junges Leben bis hierher allein so einsam zugebracht. Zuerst war ich bei meinen Eltern, nämlich sechs Jahre, auf der Farm. Meine Kinder sind aufgewachsen; sie mußten geschult werden, die Schule war weit ab, so bin ich mit mir zu Rat gegangen. Kann alle Sonntag und alle Abend bei dem Gebet getröstet werden und so bin ich mit meinen Kindern zu der Gemeinde gegangen, sie sind in die Schule gegangen und haben sehr leicht gelernt. Meine Tochter ist schon seit vier Jahren und sechs Monaten verheiratet mit einen gewissen Jakob Wurz. Sie haben drei Kinder, einen Sohn und zwei Töchter. Mein Jakob ist seit dem vergangenen Januar verheiratet mit meinem Onkel Jakob Walters Tochter Elisabeth. Mein jüngster Sohn ist noch ledig. Er ist 20 Jahre alt.

Werte Tante, haben in der Rundschau gelesen von Moses Stahl. Der liebe Onkel ist nicht mehr am Leben. Er ist schon lange tot. Er war meines Vaters Bruder; nämlich Paul Stahl. Mein lieber Vater ist auch schon lange tot. Er ist noch in Rußland gestorben. Ich war noch ein Kind von fünf Jahren. Meine liebe Mutter nahm dann ihren Schwager Johann Wipf zum Manne. Sie sind schon beide seit fünf Jahren tot. Sind nur ein Jahr auseinander gestorben. Der

David Waldner ist auch noch am Leben, aber seine Frau ist schon tot. Er wohnt in Manitoba, Canada, bei seinem jüngsten Sohn. Er hat bloß zwei Söhne. Der Johann Wurz lebt noch, er hat schon die zweite Frau. Er wohnt auch in einer Brüdergemeinde, 15 Meilen von uns ab. Seine Kinder von Deiner Schwester sind verheiratet bis auf die jüngste Tochter.

Schließe mein einfältiges Schreiben und grüße Euch, liebe Tante samt Deine[m] Mann und Kinder[n].

Verbleibe Deines Vetters tiefbetrübt[e] Frau,
Sarah Wollmann

APPENDIX III: PHOTOS

Sarah's mother Kathrina Stahl Wipf (nee Hofer), and step-father Johannes Wipf.
PHOTO COURTESY OF DELSIE HOFER.

Top: Sarah's wedding dress, side and back view. Bottom: Sarah's baptismal dress. Modeled by great-great granddaughter Tamara Wollman.

Johannes and Kathrina Wipf, with daughter Maria Knells and Maria's son Jake Knells, ca. 1906. PHOTO COURTESY OF DELSIE HOFER.

Sarah's half brother Jacob (Knox) Wipf and wife Susanna Glanzer Wipf.
PHOTO COURTESY OF DELSIE HOFER.

House that Sarah's mother and step-father lived in, near the James River.
PHOTO COURTESY OF DELSIE HOFER.

Sarah's half sister Maria Wipf Knells with husband Joseph Knells and family. (Two men are sons-in-law) circa 1923. PHOTO COURTESY OF E. ANNIE WALTER.

Sarah's sister Katrina with husband Paul C. Gross, Sarah's half-sister Maria with husband Joseph Knells. circa 1926. PHOTO COURTESY OF E. ANNIE WALTER.

Written by Sarah on the back of the photo above: "These are my sisters, Kathrina and Maria. From Sarah F. Wollman, Beiseker, Alta." (51)
PHOTO COURTESY OF E. ANNIE WALTER.

Sarah's sister Kathrina Stahl Gross, and half-sister Maria Wipf Knells.
PHOTO COURTESY OF E. ANNIE WALTER.

Springvale Community, Alberta, March 1919.

Left to right, back row: visitor; Kathrina Wurz (Tschetter, AB), Susanna Gross (West Bench, S (Huxley, AB), Rachel Gross (Ferrybank, AB); **front:** David Wipf (Prairieview, AB), Maria Wurz (

Kathrina Wurz, Susanna Wurz (back row), and Maria Wurz (front row) are Sarah's granddaughte

...s (Riverview, SK), Kathrina Tschetter (Erskine, AB), Susanna Wurz (Warburg, AB), Maria Wurz

Sarah's half-brother Jacob (nicknamed Knox) Wipf with her full brother Johannes Stahl. PHOTO COURTESY OF DELSIE HOFER.

Page 4 — Mennonitische Rundschau und Herold der Wahrheit — May 23, 1906

Nachts des Salomonos Bette, Gold aus Ophir gleich den Steinen, Würde das nicht Segen scheinen?, Doch ist's klein, wenn wir's erwägen, Nach der Himmelsgüter Segen.

Ja, Gott hat uns gesegnet mit allerlei geistlichem Segen in himmlischen Gütern durch Christum. Eph. 1, 3. Die geistlichen Güter sind edler als die leiblichen und die himmlischen höher als die irdischen, und der Segen in Christo größer als der in den Geschöpfen. O, wie sollen wir dem lieben himmlischen Vater danken für so einen köstlichen Segen, den wir schon hier genießen. Wir als Gottes Kinder sollen auch aufs neue grünen, blühen und viel Frucht bringen. Der Herr schenke es uns allen überall, wo sich seine Kinder befinden.

So weit ich weiß, sind jetzt alle gesund.

Vom 10. bis zum 13. soll hier bei uns die nördliche Konferenz sein, lade alle herzlich ein.

Noch einen herzlichen Gruß an den Editor und alle Rundschuleser, Euer geringer Pilger nach Zion,
Kornelius Ewert.

Butterischer Bruderhof, den 14. Mai 1906. Werter Editor! Bitte mein Schreiben in die Spalten der „Rundschau" aufzunehmen. Die Gnade unseres Herrn Jesu Christo sei mit uns und Euch allen. Liebe Freunde! Dieweil Ihr neugierig seid von Eurer Freundschaft zu hören, so bin ich bereit zu antworten. Ich habe in der „Rundschau" gelesen, daß Du meines Mannes Tante, Elisabeth Martens, nach meinem verschollenen Mann, Franz Wallmann, fragtest und daß meine Kinder Euch sollen Nachricht geben von ihrem Vater. Meine armen Kinder kennen ja ihren Vater nicht und wissen nichts von ihm, ich habe drei Kinder, eine Tochter Katharina und zwei Söhne, Jakob und Franz. Die Tochter weiß ein wenig von ihrem Vater, sie war vier Jahre alt, die Söhne wissen nichts von ihm, einer war drei Jahre alt; der jüngste war acht Monate alt. Ich habe meine Kinder sehr schwer und in Traurigkeit mit viel Weinen und Beten, und mit einem schweren Gemüt aufgezogen, aber Gott sei's gedankt, sie waren artig und folgsam. Die Frauen sagten oft zu mir: Du hast gute Kinder.

Pfingsten ist wieder vor der Thür

Franz berichten. Ich habe bis auf den heutigen Tag noch keine Spur und keine Nachricht von ihm wo er geblieben ist, ob er noch wo lebt oder ob er tot ist — das ist allein Gott bekannt; wäre er gestorben, so wüßte ich doch, daß ich ihn begraben hätte, aber jetzt weiß ich nichts, kann ihn nicht aus dem Sinn und Gedanken lassen, manche Leute sagen er sei tot, manche sagen er lebt — er kann sich wo aufhalten, aber er läßt nichts von sich hören. Das glaube ich nicht eher, bis ich ihn mit meinen leiblichen Augen sehen werde, daß er noch lebt. O wie gerne möchte ich schon Auskunft von ihm haben, denn es kann ja ein jeder denken, wie es einem ums Herz ist, aber es fühlt's nur der, den es betrifft. Ich habe ein schweres Herz und Gemüt schon so viele Jahre, wenn's mir der liebe Heiland nicht thät tragen helfen, so könnte ich es nicht durchmachen, aber er ist ja gnädig und barmherzig gegen seine Kinder, die ihn lieben und ihm vertrauen, denen hilft er ja überwinden.

Es ist jetzt 19 Jahre und 6 Monate daß mein Franz nach Rußland gereist und nicht mehr zurückgekommen ist. Sein Onkel, der Andreas Wallmann hat mir vor vielen Jahren Nachricht gegeben, daß mein Franz bis nach New York gekommen ist und von dort ein Ticket genommen, um nach Freeman zu fahren, aber abgefahren wäre er nicht. So muß er wahrscheinlich in der bösen Stadt geblieben sein. Das Sprichwort sagt wohl: Es ist kein Faden so fein gesponnen und nichts Heimliches, das nicht offenbar wird," aber von der traurigen Geschichte ist bis jetzt noch nichts ans Licht gekommen! — Bitte wenn jemand etwas von ihm weiß, der möchte es mir berichten und zu wissen thun.

Dein Bruder Jakob ist mit seinen drei Kindern in der Brüdergemeinde, zwei Söhne hat er verheiratet und der jüngste ist noch ledig, er und seine Frau sehen schon alt aus, sie sind dieses Frühjahr 100 Meilen weitergezogen, sowie auch 16 andere Familien und haben eine Gemeinde angelegt in Beadel County. Deine Mutter und Schwestern Susanna und Katharina, sind nicht mehr am Leben, Dein Bruder Abraham ist weit ab von uns, nämlich in Manitoba, Canada mit seinen Kindern und die Dariasleute

Kindern, nämlich bei den Darlasleuten. Ich bin jetzt schon 14 Jahre in der Gemeinde. Im natürlichen Leben geht es mir nichts ab, wir haben von allem genug, nur das eine fehlt, daß ich nicht weiß wo mein Mann geblieben ist. Als er nach Rußland reiste, war ich 23 Jahre alt und den 19. Juni werde ich 43 Jahre alt, habe also mit Gottes Hilfe mein junges Leben bis hierher allein so einsam zugebracht. Zuerst war ich bei meinen Eltern, nämlich sechs Jahre, auf der Farm. Meine Kinder sind aufgewachsen; sie mußten geschult werden, die Schule war weit ab, so bin ich mit nicht zu Rat gegangen. Kann alle Sonntag und alle Abend bei dem Gebet getröstet werden und bin ich mit meinen Kindern zu der Gemeinde gegangen, sie sind in die Schule gegangen und haben sehr viel gelernt; meine Tochter ist schon seit vier Jahren und sechs Monaten verheiratet mit einem gewissen Jakob Wurz, sie haben drei Kinder, einen Sohn und zwei Töchter. Mein Jakob ist seit dem vergangenen Januar verheiratet mit meines Onkels Jakob Walters Tochter Elisabeth. Mein jüngster Sohn ist noch ledig, er ist 20 Jahre alt.

Werte Tante, haben in der Rundschau gelesen von Moses Stahl, der liebe Onkel ist nicht mehr am Leben, er ist schon lange tot, er war meines Vaters Bruder nämlich Paul Stahl. Mein lieber Vater ist auch schon lange tot, er ist noch in Rußland gestorben, ich war noch in Rußland die fünf Jahre. Meine liebe Mutter nahm dann ihren Schwager Johann Wipf zum Manne, sie sind schon beide seit fünf Jahren tot, sind nur ein Jahr auseinander gestorben. Der David Waldner ist noch am Leben, aber seine Frau schon tot, er wohnt in Manitoba, Canada, bei seinem jüngsten Sohn; er hat bloß zwei Söhne. Der Johann Wurz lebt noch, er hat schon die zweite Frau, er wohnt auch in einer Brüdergemeinde, 15 Meilen von uns ab, seine Kinder von Deiner Schwester sind verheiratet bis auf die jüngste Tochter.

Schließe mein einfältiges Schreiben und grüße Euch, liebe Tante, sammt Deinen Mann und Kinder. Verbleibe Deines Vetters tiefbetrübte Frau,
Sarah Wallmann.

Sarah's letter, as published in the *Mennonitische Rundschau*, May 23, 1906.
IMAGE COURTESY OF CENTRE FOR MENNONITE BRETHREN STUDIES.

A sign in rural Saskatchewan. The Hutterite journey continues…descendants of Frank and Sarah Wollman have settled in many places across Canada and the United States. This road leads to Lost River Colony near Allan, Saskatchewan.
PHOTO COURTESY OF MICHAEL WOLLMAN.

www.ingramcontent.com/pod-product-compliance
Lightning Source LLC
Chambersburg PA
CBHW041132110526
44592CB00020B/2780